JOURNEY THROUGH
ITALY

ANITA GANERI

W
FRANKLIN WATTS

Franklin Watts
Published in Great Britain in 2018 by The Watts Publishing Group

Credits
Editor in Chief: John Miles
Series Editor: Amy Stephenson
Series Designer: Emma DeBanks
Picture Researcher: Diana Morris

Picture Credits: Alexandrpeers/Dreamstime: 7bla. Andreykr/Dreamstime: 12. argalis/istockphoto: 11t. Axiom/Superstock: 6cr. Caterina Belova/Shutterstock: 6br, 29c. Tatiana Belova/Dreamstime: 19t. Thomas Bethge/Shutterstock: 7b. Paulo Bona/Shutterstock: 21bl. Bopra77/Shutterstock: 7bcr. Roberto Cancino/Dreamstime: 23t. Gandolfo Cannatella/Shutterstock: 15c. Chaoss/Dreamstime: 19c. Angelo Cordeschi/Dreamstime: 7tcbl. Cubo Images/Superstock: 17. Christain Delbert Dreamstime: 7tcb. Duskbabe/Dreamstime: 7tcr. Ebastard129/Dreamstime: 6cl, 15b. Harry Engels/Getty Images: 22c. De Fillipo/Dreamstime: 3, 16c. Gamma-Rapho/Getty Images: 8. Remus Grigore/Dreamstime: 7tr. Eduardo Grundi/Superstock: 21br. Bruno Haver/Dreamstime: 7tc. Ilfede/Dreamstime: 11c. Matej Kastelic/Shutterstock: 5b. Katatonia82/Dreamstime: 21t. Brenda Kean/Dreamstime: 16b. Ian Keirle/Dreamstime: 9b. Alexander Kosarev/Shutterstock: 25t. Andy Kuzmin/Shutterstock: 7cbr. lapas77/Shutterstock: 13t. leoks/Shutterstock: 27t. Viacheslav Lopatin/Shutterstock: 5t. Lunamarina/Dreamstime: 7ba. mary416/Shutterstock: 11b. Mikadun/Shutterstock: 6tc, 13b. Minerva Studio/Shutterstock: 25b. minnystock/Dreamstime: 18-19 John Pavel/Dreamstime: 20. William Perry/Dreamstime: 7ca. Photoeuphoria/Dreamstime: 7bca. I Pilou/Shutterstock: 6bl, 23b. Mauro Dalla Pozza/Dreamstime: 10. QQ7/Shutterstock: 1. M Rohana/Shutterstock: 27b. Route 66/Shutterstock: 7cbl. Salajean/Dreamstime: 6tl, 9t. Sborisov/Dreamstime: front cover, 4. Anastasia Shapochkina/Dreamstime: 7c. Elena Shchipkova/Shutterstock: 29t. Samuel Strickler/Dreamstime: 22b. Studiogi/Dreamstime: 24. Swinnerrr/Dreamstime: 6tr. 7tca. Richard Thomas/Dreamstime: 7tl. Dmitry Vereshchagin/Shutterstock: 7tcl. V Voevale/Dreamstime: 28-29. Taras Vyshnya/Shutterstock: 26. Andreas Zerndl/Dreamstime: 14.

Dewey number: 945
HB ISBN: 978 1 4451 3667 7

Printed in China

Franklin Watts
An imprint of
Hachette Children's Group
Part of The Watts Publishing Group
Carmelite House
50 Victoria Embankment
London EC4Y 0DZ

An Hachette UK Company
www.hachette.co.uk
www.franklinwatts.co.uk

CONTENTS

WELCOME TO ITALY!

Benvenuti in Italia! Welcome to Italy! Covering an area of around 301,268 sq km, Italy is a beautiful country in southern Europe, with an incredibly rich artistic and cultural history. When you think of Italy, you might imagine pizza, pasta, sports cars and football. But there's much more to Italy than that. On this journey, you'll be taking a tour of ancient ruins, marvelling at priceless paintings, climbing in the mountains, and riding a gondola in Venice – a unique city set in a lagoon.

Mountains, islands and volcanoes

Italy is a long, boot-shaped country, jutting out into the Mediterranean Sea. To the north, it is divided from the rest of Europe by the vast sweep of the Alps mountains. The central regions are characterised by rolling hills and the Apennines mountains. To the south, it includes the large islands of Sardinia and Sicily (with its active volcano) as well as many smaller islands.

▼ Nearly two-thirds of Tuscany (a region in central Italy) is covered by a hilly landscape.

Story of Italy

Italy was home to the ancient Romans who built a mighty empire, centred on the city of Rome. Rome also became important for early Christians, especially after the Roman Emperor Constantine converted to Christianity in the 4th century CE. After the fall of Rome, Italy's history was mainly one of unrest as small, independent states battled against each other. It was not until 1871 that Italy was united, with Rome as its capital.

▲ The Colosseum in Rome is one of Italy's most iconic Roman buildings.

Life in Italy

Today, Italy has 20 regions, each with its own traditions and culture. The north of Italy is more industrial and much wealthier than the south. Across the whole country, three passions run through Italian life: family, food and football. Italians are warm and welcoming, and love to relax around a table at home or in a restaurant with their extended family and friends.

Parli Italiano?

Do you speak Italian? Italian is the official language of Italy. Here are a few useful phrases to help you on your journey.

- *Ciao* – hi/hello/goodbye
- *Buongiorno* – good morning
- *Buonasera* – good evening
- *Buonanotte* – good night
- *Per favore* – please
- *Grazie* – thank you
- *Molto lieto* – pleased to meet you
- *Quanto costa?* – how much is this?
- *Mi scusi* – I'm sorry/excuse me
- *Non capisco* – I don't understand

◀ Italians love to combine food with socialising!

5

YOUR JOURNEY

JOURNEY PLANNER

The A

Aosta

5

T

1

2

FRANCE

3

4

SPAIN

5

Mediterranean Sea

KEY

———	your route around Italy
-------	flight / ferry
———	river
———	road
★	capital city

6

AUSTRIA

Brenner Pass

1

The Dolomites

Bolzano

Trento

Lake Como
Lake Garda

Rovereto

Bergamo

Milan

Brescia

Valpolicella

Treviso

Vicenza

Venice **2**

SLOVENIA

HUNGARY

SERBIA

CROATIA

Pavia

Verona

Padova

Piacénza

Parma

Ferrara

BOSNIA
HERZEGOVINA

Maranello

Modena

Bologna

Ravenna

Genoa

Prato

Forli

Rimini

MONTENEGRO

Pisa

Florence

Ancona

Adriatic Sea

Livorno

Siena

Lake Trasimeno

Perugia

Lake Bolsena

Terni

Pescara

Lake Varano

CORSICA

Lake Bracciano

L'Aquila

Vatican City

Rome

6

Latina

Campobasso

Foggia

Bari

Lecce

Caserta

Naples

4

Pompeii

Salerno

Potenza

Taranto

Tyrrhenian Sea

SARDINIA

Sassari

Nuoro

Cosenza

Catanzaro

Cagliari

Messina

Calabria

Ionian Sea

Palermo

3

Mount Etna

SICILY

Catania

Caltanissetta

Siracusa

Strait of Sicily

Agrigento

BRENNER PASS TO BOLZANO

Your journey starts in the far north of Italy, on a motorway high up in the Alps. You drive across the border from Austria through the Brenner Pass, at an altitude of 1,375 m. All around you are snowy peaks, green pastures and dark forests of coniferous trees. People have been using this route to cross the Alps since prehistoric times. Today, it is still one of the most important, and busiest, north to south connections through Europe.

Bolzano Bozen

Bolzano is the capital of the Trentino-Alto Adige province of northern Italy. The city lies in a valley, where two rivers (the Iscaro and the Talvera) meet. Its German name is Bozen and, throughout its history, control of this region has passed back and forth between Austria and Italy. Today, the city is home to both German and Italian speakers. Bolzano is also home to Ötzi, a 5,300-year-old mummy. You can visit Ötzi in the South Tyrol Museum of Archaeology, and see the clothes, shoes and equipment found with his body.

The discovery of Ötzi

In 1991, two German hikers walking high up in the Ötztal Alps noticed something lying in a gully below. Sticking out of the ice and snow were the head and shoulders of a human body. The hikers thought they had found the frozen remains of a dead climber. They took a photo and reported their find. But when the body was recovered, it soon became clear that this was the mummified corpse of a man who had lived thousands of years ago. The mummy had been preserved beneath the glacial ice. The man was nicknamed Ötzi, after the mountains in which he was found.

◀ Ötzi was visited by famous climbers Hans Kammerlander and Reinhold Messner two days after he was discovered by hikers.

▲ The Dolomites are named after the type of rock they are made from – dolomite.

The Dolomites

From Bolzano, it's easy to take a trip into the mountains that lie on either side of the valley. These are the Dolomites, immense slabs of rock that have been sculpted by ice, sun and rain into soaring spires and jagged ridges. Many people visit the Dolomites for their dramatic scenery, and to ski, walk and climb. The area is also famous for its *via ferratas* (iron roads) – paths for people with a good head for heights. These mountain routes have steel safety wires fixed into the rock for climbers to use. There are ladders and bridges, too. Just don't look down!

▲ A young climber braves a via ferrata route in the Dolomites.

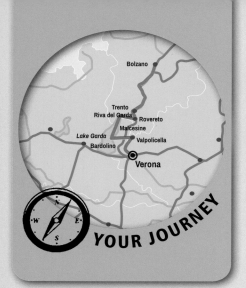

BOLZANO TO VERONA

From Bolzano, head south on the train. Just south of the town of Rovereto, break your journey to visit some unusual footprints. Around 200 million years ago, dinosaurs roamed this region – although the landscape was very different at that time. The dinosaurs left trails of footprints in the muddy shoreline of a vast ocean, called the Thetys Sea. Some have survived as footprint fossils in the rocks.

Lake Garda

Next, jump onto a bus to Riva del Garda, a popular resort on beautiful Lake Garda. It's the largest lake in Italy and a brilliant place for windsurfing and sailing, thanks to the winds that blow from the north every morning, and from the south every afternoon. You can hop onto a fast hydrofoil to travel down the lake to Malcesine. Here, take a ride on the cableway to the top of Monte Baldo, which is 1,745 m high. As the cableway goes up, it slowly rotates, giving you spectacular views along the whole length of the lake.

▶ Windsurfing is a popular tourist activity on Lake Garda.

Wine

Your journey continues by bus through the vineyards of the Bardolino and Valpolicella regions. Wine-making is a very old tradition in Italy. It is the second biggest producer of wine in the world after France. Vines were first grown by the ancient Greeks, and the ancient Romans developed wine-making, spreading it throughout their empire. Each wine-growing region in Italy produces its own varieties and flavours depending on the type of soil, climate and landscape.

▲ A vineyard in the Valpolicella region.

Verona

Your bus will arrive in the centre of Verona at the busy Piazza delle Erbe. Verona was an important ancient Roman settlement, and there are many impressive ruins. A short walk through the medieval streets takes you to the enormous amphitheatre, which was completed in 30 CE. It could hold up to 30,000 people, who flocked to watch bloody combats as gladiators fought to the death.

Romeo and Juliet

Verona is the setting for William Shakespeare's play *Romeo and Juliet*. Shakespeare based his play on a story written in the 1520s about two lovers from rival families, the Capulets and the Montagues. While the two families did exist in real life, Romeo and Juliet are fictional characters. Nevertheless, one of the most popular attractions in Verona is a stone balcony, like the one where Juliet and Romeo meet in secret (see above).

▼ Today the amphitheatre is used to stage operas, concerts and host pop and rock musicians on tour.

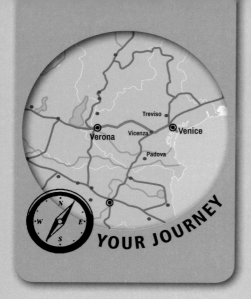

YOUR JOURNEY

VERONA TO VENICE

The quickest way to get from Verona to Venice is by *Frecciargento* (high-speed train). It takes one hour to make the 115 km journey. As you walk out of Santa Lucia station, you can't miss the Grand Canal directly in front of you. This is the main canal that flows through Venice. Take a *vaporetto* (water bus) on route 1 to travel the length of the Grand Canal.

The Grand Canal

Venice is a city built on three main islands and 114 smaller islands. It has 177 canals, and all of this lies in the Venetian Lagoon. The Grand Canal is wide and very busy. Everything moves by water here. As you make your way down the canal, look out for police boats, fire boats, water taxis, boats loaded up with goods and boats collecting rubbish. See if you can spot the traditional gondolas (see page 13) ferrying tourists around the sights of Venice.

Rialto Bridge

Rounding a corner, the vaporetto takes you underneath the most famous of the Grand Canal's four bridges – the Rialto. Built in 1591, for many centuries this was the only way to cross the Grand Canal by foot. The bridge linked the bustling commercial heart of the city, and today this area is still home to busy meat, fish and vegetable markets.

▼ The Rialto Bridge is one of only four bridges that cross the Grand Canal in Venice.

▶ At 99 m, the bell tower of Saint Mark's Basilica is the tallest building in Venice.

Art galleries

The buildings that line the Grand Canal include beautiful churches and palaces. Many of the palaces are now museums, art galleries or expensive hotels. Art-lovers should drop in to the Accademia Gallery. Here you can see works by many great artists, including Canaletto – famous for his paintings of Venice in the 1700s. Just along the Grand Canal from the Accademia is the Peggy Guggenheim Collection, with its collections of modern art.

Piazza San Marco

End your day at Saint Mark's Basilica, (located in the Piazza San Marco) a sumptuous church that was built in the 11th century. You can also visit the exquisite Doge's Palace. The doges were once the rulers of Venice, and this palace was their home, as well as the centre of Venice's government.

The gondoliers

Gondolas, piloted by gondoliers, used to be the main means of transporting goods around Venice before motorised boats took over. In the past, Venice was an important port where goods from all over the world were imported and exported. Today, gondolas are mainly used by tourists to cross the Grand Canal or to take a tour around Venice. Gondoliers have to pass an exam that tests their historical knowledge, language skills and of course their gondola-handling skills!

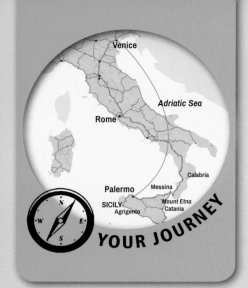

YOUR JOURNEY

VENICE TO PALERMO

A short flight from Venice's Marco Polo airport takes you to your next destination – Palermo, on the island of Sicily. Alternatively, you could take the train south to Rome, then continue along the wild and beautiful coast of Calabria, the 'toe' of Italy, before catching a ferry. Be prepared for a long journey, though – it takes 15 hours and covers more than 1,400 km.

Sicily

Sicily is the largest island in the Mediterranean Sea, and lies off the south-west tip of Italy's 'toe'. During its long history, it has been conquered and ruled by many different peoples, including the Greeks, Romans, Arabs, Normans, Spanish and French. Each has left a mark on the island, from the ancient Greek remains of the 'Valley of the Temples' to the great Norman cathedral at Monreale, just south of Palermo.

▶ The interior of the Monreale Cathedral is decorated with beautiful and intricate mosaics.

Holiday spot

With its rich history, stunning scenery and sunny climate, Sicily is a popular holiday destination. As well as receiving visitors from abroad, many Italian tourists visit from mainland Italy. Summers can be very hot so it's best to head to one of the island's main beaches, where cooling breezes take the edge off the heat. You can also visit the volcanic Aeolian Islands, off the north coast.

Mount Etna

At 3,329 m, Mount Etna is the highest and most active volcano in Europe. It rises high above the landscape in the east of Sicily, and erupts almost constantly. Despite the dangers, many people have settled on Etna's slopes because the fertile soil is good for growing oranges, lemons, olives and vines. One of the best ways to see the volcano from all sides is to take the 110-km trip on the Circumetnea Railway – a historic line that takes you around the volcano through the villages, farms and old lava flows.

▼ Mount Etna ejects a plume of smoke and ash in 2012.

Street food

If you're feeling peckish by the time you reach Palermo, why not sample some of the city's famous street food?

- *Arancini* – fried balls of rice filled with meat and peas

- *Sfincioni* (Sicilian pizza) – soft bread topped with tomato, onions, and cheese (see below)

- *Cazilli* – potato croquettes with parsley

- *Panelle* – chickpea fritters

- *Pane ca meusa* – a soft roll filled with fried calf's spleen and lung

15

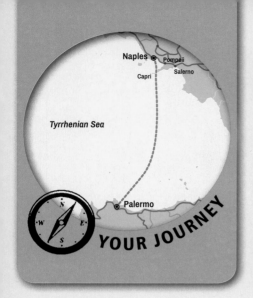

YOUR JOURNEY

PALERMO TO NAPLES

A relaxing way to get back to the mainland is by ferry, from Palermo to the city of Naples. On the way, you'll pass the beautiful island of Capri, a favourite holiday destination since ancient Roman times. Emperor Tiberius built several palaces and villas on the island. Today, Capri is still visited by thousands of tourists every year.

A busy port

Naples is the capital of the Italian region of Campania, and the third largest city in Italy, after Rome and Milan. Your ferry docks in the port of Naples, one of the busiest in the Mediterranean, among towering cruise ships, and container ships and tankers that daily carry large amounts of cargo in and out of the port.

A treasure trove

A short ride on the underground railway takes you to one of the top archaeological museums in the world. Naples' National Archaeological Museum (see right) contains many treasures from ancient times, including a large collection of Greek and Roman sculptures, Roman mosaics, and many other objects including vases, glassware and jewellery. Many of these items come from nearby Pompeii and Herculaneum (see pages 18–19).

▲ Mount Vesuvius dominates the landscape of the 15-kilometre-wide Bay of Naples.

▲ The classic pizza margherita topping echoes the Italian flag, with its green basil, white mozzarella and red tomatoes.

Pizza heaven

You won't go hungry in Naples – home of the pizza! Naples was once an ancient Greek settlement, which was later taken over by the Romans. A simple Greek dish of flat bread, topped with oil and herbs evolved over the centuries in Naples into the pizza we know today.

Traditional Neapolitan pizza is made with soft, light dough, expertly stretched by a master *pizzaiolo* (pizza-maker) and cooked in a very hot wood-burning brick oven for just 90 seconds. Head for the world's first pizza restaurant, Antica Pizzeria Port'Alba, which opened in Naples in 1830, and is still serving delicious pizzas today.

Other places to visit

- MADRE – the Museum of Modern Art, opened in 2005. Highlights are works by artists such as Andy Warhol and Damien Hirst.

- The *centro storico* 'historic centre' – walk through the narrow, busy streets around *Via dei Tribunali* (the main street that runs from east to west) to get a feel for life in Naples.

- Cappella Sansevero – a tiny chapel where you'll find an extraordinary marble sculpture called *The Veiled Christ*, and some rather gruesome 18th-century exhibits in human anatomy – you have been warned!

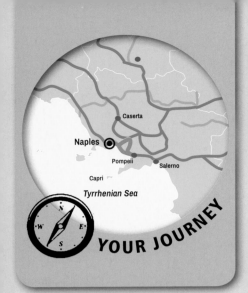

YOUR JOURNEY

POMPEII AND VESUVIUS

Mount Vesuvius, another active volcano, looms to the east of the city of Naples. At 1,281 m, Vesuvius is not as high as Mount Etna, but it is considered to be much more dangerous because far more people live close by. Its last big eruption was in 1944. Scientists warn that another eruption could happen at any time – but despite monitoring the volcano carefully, they cannot predict exactly when this will occur.

▼ Three million people live close enough to be affected by the next eruption of Mount Vesuvius.

Vesuvius eruption

In 79 CE, Vesuvius erupted spectacularly, sending a giant cloud of ash, rock and gas over 30 km into the sky. When this massive cloud collapsed, it caused a deadly avalanche of hot ash and gas that quickly overwhelmed the nearby Roman towns of Herculaneum and Pompeii. Thousands of people died, and the towns themselves were completely buried in a deep layer of ash and mud. Today, large areas of these towns have been excavated to reveal the Roman remains beneath.

Pompeii

The easiest way to take a day trip to see Pompeii and Vesuvius is to catch a train from Naples on the Circumvesuviana line. From the station, you can tour around the Roman ruins. The blanket of ash preserved the remains for almost 2,000 years before they were dug up, giving a unique glimpse into ancient Roman life. At the time of its destruction, Pompeii was a thriving, busy town with 20,000 inhabitants. Now it is one of Italy's biggest tourist attractions.

Around the crater

To go up Vesuvius itself, hop on a minibus. The road has many tight and scary hairpin bends, but as you go higher and higher, you will be rewarded with dramatic views across the Bay of Naples. To reach the top, you need to walk up a steep path across ash and rock. The path around the rim of the crater (see right) is narrow, with steep cliffs on the inside. All around, you will see the signs of past eruptions.

▼ A street in Pompeii.

What to see in Pompeii

- Forum – a large public space surrounded by official buildings and temples

- Shops – loaves were found in the ovens at the bakery of Modestus

- Villas – the walls of these luxurious houses were decorated with beautiful paintings

- Amphitheatre – with room for around 12,000 people

- Temple of Jupiter – with plaster casts of some of the victims

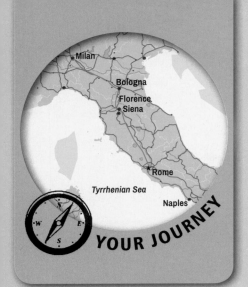

NAPLES TO MILAN

It's time to head north again, so take an overnight inter-city train from Naples to Milan. Book into a cabin and wake up at your destination. This wealthy city is the centre of business, fashion and finance in Italy so there's plenty to explore.

► Marble is a popular material for ornate buildings like the cathedral, because it is suitable for carving and sculpting intricate designs.

The Duomo

The Duomo di Milano (cathedral) dominates the Piazza del Duomo in the centre of the city. Built of marble from quarries in Mergozzo to the north of Milan, this building has an extraordinary roof – try counting the 135 spires. Work on the cathedral began in 1386, but the building took over 400 years to complete. You can climb up to the roof and take a tour around the spires and statues. You can even get a view of the Alps on a clear day.

High fashion

Fashion and design are hugely important industries in Milan, and Milan fashion weeks are a must for creative types. Stop off at one of Milan's most glittering shopping arcades, the Galleria Vittorio Emanuele II. This grand arcade has a glass and metal dome and ceiling that was designed in 1865 by the Italian architect, Guiseppe Mengoni. Sadly Mengoni fell to his death from some scaffolding days before the Galleria opened in 1877. Today, the Galleria bustles with people visiting the cafés and famous designer shops that line its walkways.

Money, money, money

Milan is Italy's business and banking powerhouse. Italy's main stock exchange is located here along with over 200 banking companies. Manufacturing, media and tourism also make a large contribution to the money pouring into this city.

San Siro Stadium

On the outskirts of Milan is the San Siro Stadium (see below), home to both of Milan's premier football teams – AC Milan and FC Internazionale Milano (Inter Milan). Football is the most popular sport in Italy, and both of Milan's teams play in *Serie A*, one of the best football leagues in the world.

▲ The Galleria is home to some of the most expensive and exclusive shops in Milan.

The *loggionisti*

No trip to Milan is complete without a visit to the famous theatre of La Scala. Many opera singers tremble at the thought of singing at La Scala because of the infamous loggionisti – opera fans who watch from the upper gallery. If they don't like what they are hearing and seeing, they let everyone know – often by booing and hissing.

▲ La Scala's famous horseshoe-shaped auditorium.

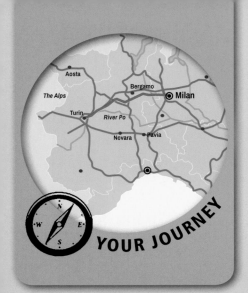

YOUR JOURNEY

MILAN TO TURIN

If you're feeling energetic, hire a bike in Milan and take a couple of days to cycle the 170 km to Turin. Follow the smaller roads and cycle paths that cross the flat plain of the River Po. Part of your journey will take you along the route of the *VenTo* – a proposed long-distance cycle path that would link Turin to Milan and Venice. At 632 km, it would be the longest cycle path in Italy.

The Giro

The route from Milan to Turin is sometimes included as part of a stage of the *Giro d'Italia*, the biggest cycling race in Italy. Along with the *Tour de France* and *la Vuelta a España* (Spain), the Giro is one of the three cycling events known as 'Grand Tours'. Teams from all over the world come to Italy to compete in the 23-day race, which takes the cyclists through the Alps and all over Italy. Each day, the leader (the rider with the fastest overall time) wears the prized bright pink jersey.

River Po

The River Po is Italy's longest river, flowing from the Alps in the west to Italy's east coast. The river's vast flood plain is very fertile and the area around Vercelli is a centre for rice growing. Your route takes you through expanses of flooded fields, filled with rice plants.

▲ Cyclist Nairo Quintana wearing the pink leader's jersey in the 2014 Giro.

◀ A view of the Alps from rice fields in Vercelli.

Turin

Turin is a centre of business and industry, lying on the edge of the River Po flood plain, in the shadow of the Alps. It is a beautiful city, with elegant streets and arcades, and many interesting churches and museums. It has also been home to the FIAT car company for over 100 years.

▼ Many buildings in Turin have red terracotta roof tiles – a traditional Italian roofing material.

The Turin Shroud

Turin Cathedral is home to one of the most famous holy relics in the world. The Turin Shroud is a linen cloth that shows the image of a crucified man. Many people believe that it is the cloth in which Jesus Christ was wrapped after his death on the cross. The shroud is only rarely displayed to the public, but you can visit the Museum of the Shroud, which will tell you all about it.

▲ A detail of the Turin Shroud, which shows an image of a man's face.

YOUR JOURNEY

TURIN TO BOLOGNA

From Turin, a high-speed *Frecciarossa* train will take you to the city of Bologna in just over two hours. Bologna lies in the Emilia-Romagna region of Italy, which has a reputation as a centre of gastronomy (the study of food) so you're in for a treat if you like Italian food.

Regional specialities

On the journey, you'll pass through several places with names associated with food. Parma is famous for its fine *prosciutto* (ham) and for *Parmigiano-Reggiano* (Parmesan) cheese, while balsamic vinegar is produced around Modena. You'll also see many vineyards, used to produce the famous, fizzy Lambrusco wine.

▼ Pasta, cured meat, wine, balsamic vinegar and cheese are all classic ingredients used in Italian recipes.

► A classic Ferrari Formula 1 racing car.

Sports cars

The region is also famous for being the centre of sports car production. It is home to several of the top car makers, including Ferrari, Lamborghini and Maserati. Enzo Ferrari was born in Maranello, near Modena, and today people come from all over the world to visit the Ferrari Museum in the town. Ferruccio Lamborghini was born in a small village near Bologna and today Lamborghinis are built in nearby Ferrara. Maserati was founded in Bologna. Its trident logo was inspired by a statue of Neptune (the Roman god of the sea) in the city.

'La grassa'

Bologna's nickname in Italy is 'la grassa' – 'the fat one' – because of its links to food. Local specialities include *mortadella* (cooked pork salami), hand-made pasta, such as tortellini, lasagne and tagliatelli; and the delicious Bolognese sauce (*ragu*), made from minced beef, tomato paste and vegetables. Just off the Piazza Maggiore, you'll find the old medieval market and food shopping area. Here you can taste and buy food from shops that have been selling Bologna's specialities for generations.

Spaghetti Bolognese?

Although it is probably the best-known Italian dish outside Italy, you won't find spaghetti on the menu in Bologna. Bolognese sauce is served with many types of pasta in the city, especially tagliatelle and lasagne, but never with spaghetti! In fact, spaghetti is made from a different type of wheat grown in the south of Italy, around Naples. It is too slippery for the Bolognese sauce, which is much better served with wider pasta shapes.

◄ A shopkeeper in Bologna shows off his mortadella.

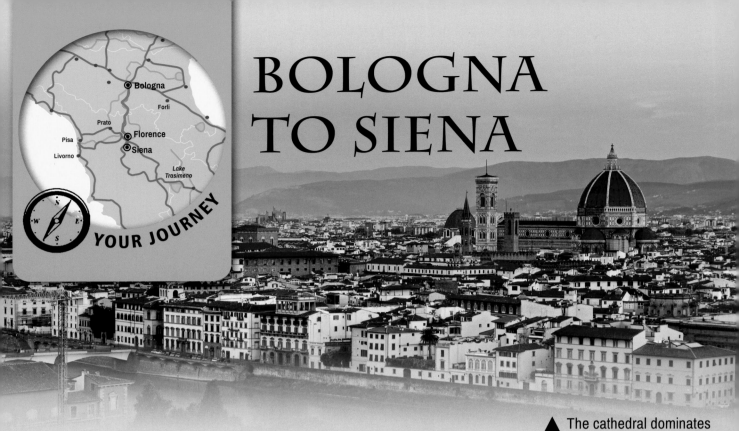

BOLOGNA TO SIENA

The cathedral dominates the Florence skyline.

From Bologna, head south through Tuscany, famous for its beautiful landscapes, art and history. Take the Autostrada 1 as far as Florence – a motorway that winds its way through the Apennine mountains. In fact, the road is so narrow and twisting that a new, more direct route has been under construction for the past 10 years. When it is completed, the new A1 motorway will include 23 viaducts and 22 new tunnels.

Florence

In medieval times, Florence was a commercial centre. Its most powerful family, the Medicis, made their fortune from banking. In the 15th century, Florence was the birthplace of the Renaissance movement, and today it is one of the great artistic and cultural capitals of the world. Start your tour with the city's tallest building – the Duomo (cathedral). This multi-coloured and patterned building is topped with a massive dome. Designed by the Italian architect Filippo Brunelleschi, when it was completed in 1463, the dome was the largest in the world.

The treasures of Florence

- The Uffizi Gallery – home to some of the finest Renaissance masterpieces, collected by the Medici family

- The Baptistery – the oldest building in Florence

- *Ponte Vecchio* (Old Bridge) – a shop-lined bridge built in 1345 across the River Arno

- Piazza della Signoria – the central square in Florence. Look for Michelangelo's famous statue of David.

Tower rivalry

From Florence, hop back in the car to head towards Siena. On the way you'll spot San Gimignano (see right) quite some time before you arrive in this beautiful hilltop town. That's because of the 14 towers that dot its skyline. These towers are all that survive of 72 towers, built by rival noble families in the 13th and 14th centuries to display their power and wealth. You can visit one of the towers – the Torre Grossa, built in 1311 – and climb the 54 m to the top for great views of the tiled rooftops and countryside below.

Siena

When you arrive in Siena, head for the main square – the Piazza del Campo – a fan-shaped area paved with red brick. This is where the famous horse races, known as the *Palio*, are held every summer. These races date back to medieval times, and the ten riders race bareback at full tilt around the piazza. It's quite common for a jockey to be thrown off and his horse to finish the race without a rider.

▼ In the Palio, each pairing of horse and rider represents a different *contrade* (city district) of Siena.

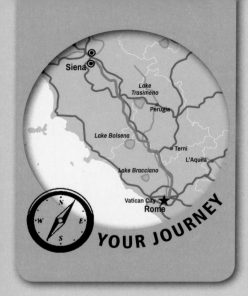

YOUR JOURNEY

SIENA TO ROME

To end your journey, take a long walk along an ancient pilgrimage way. The Via Francigena was traditionally a pilgrimage route, starting in the cathedral city of Canterbury, England, and making its way through France to its final destination in Rome, the capital of Italy. From Siena, you'll walk the southern section, which will take you past the scenic lakes of Bolsena and Bracciano.

Vatican City

The pilgrimage route ends at St Peter's Basilica in Rome. Strictly speaking, St Peter's isn't in Italy at all. It is in Vatican City, the world's smallest independent state (less than half a square km), which lies within the city of Rome. This is the headquarters of the Roman Catholic Church, and home of the Pope, leader of the world's Catholics. St Peter's is one of the world's largest churches. Its massive dome was designed by Michelangelo to rival the cathedral dome in Florence (see page 26).

▼ St Peter's Basilica is located at the western end of St Peter's Square.

Exploring the Vatican

To get to St Peter's, you will walk through a massive, circular piazza. On religious festivals and special occasions, this area is crammed with people who come from all over the world to be blessed by the Pope from a balcony at the front of St Peter's. Here you'll also find the Vatican Museums. They are home to priceless art collections, as well as the famous Sistine Chapel – with its beautiful ceiling frescoes by Michelangelo (1475–1564).

◀ Beyond St Peter's and Vatican City lies the city of Rome.

Old and new

Finish your Italian journey with a visit to some ancient Roman remains in the centre of Rome – the Forum, the famous Colosseum (see page 5), the Pantheon and the baths of Diocletian, the largest public baths in ancient Rome. If you prefer something more modern, visit Cinecittà – the largest film studios in Europe and the heart of Italy's booming film industry. All that sightseeing is hot work, so cool down with a refreshing *gelato* (ice cream) from one of Rome's many gelateria (see right).

Religion in Italy

Italy is a largely Roman Catholic country, with Catholics making up more than 80 per cent of the population. The Pope is not only the head of the Catholic Church worldwide, but also the Bishop of Rome. There are other religious minorities in Italy too, including Orthodox Christian, Muslim and Jewish communities.

GLOSSARY

altitude
Height above sea level.

amphitheatre
An open-air, oval or circular arena with seats in tiers all the way round and a central performance area, used for entertainment and sport in ancient Roman times.

Apennines
A mountain range that extends along the length of Italy, from Altare in the Alps to Reggio Calabria at the 'toe' of the mainland.

Carthaginian
Describes people from Carthage, a city in modern-day Tunisia that was the centre of the ancient Carthaginian civilisation.

duomo
The Italian word for cathedral.

fall of Rome
The end of the Roman Empire in Western Europe. The last emperor was Romulus Augustulus and he was overthrown in 476 CE.

fritter
A type of fried food, often covered in batter or breadcrumbs.

gladiator
An armed fighter who fought other gladiators or wild animals, to entertain crowds in ancient Roman times. Some gladiators were volunteers, but many were slaves, and they often fought to the death.

gondola
A traditional, flat-bottomed boat found in Venice, which is pushed along by one long rowing oar, worked by the gondolier standing near the back of the boat.

Grand Tours
In competitive cycling, the three Grand Tours are the Tour de France, the Giro d'Italia and the Vuelta a Espāna.

hydrofoil
A type of boat with fins beneath that lift the hull out of the water when it is travelling at speed.

Jewish
Describes someone who is a member of the Jewish faith, either by birth or because they have converted to Judaism.

Lagoon
A stretch of salt water that is separated from the sea by a low sandbank or coral reef.

Michelangelo
An Italian painter, sculptor and architect, born in 1475 and died in 1564. He is considered to be one of the greatest Western artists of all time.

mosaic
A pattern or picture made up from many small pieces of coloured stone or glass.

mummified
A body (usually of a person) that has been preserved so the body does not rot.

Muslim
A person who follows the religion of Islam.

Orthodox Christian
A member of one of the three main Christian groups (the other two being Roman Catholic and Protestant).

piazza
A public square or marketplace in an Italian town or city.

pilgrimage
A journey made to a place that is special to a religion, such as a saint's shrine.

relic
In religion, a bone or similar item from the body of a saint or holy person, which is treasured and worshipped.

Renaissance
A period in European history following the Middle Ages, from about 1350 to 1600, which started in Italy and spread across Europe, when the arts and science flourished.

shroud
A cloth that covers and protects a dead body.

stock exchange
A place where stocks, shares and other financial services are bought and sold.

terracotta
A type of clay, used to make tiles and pottery, which often has a deep golden-brown colour.

trident
A spear with three points on the end. The god Neptune is often shown holding a trident.

viaduct
A long bridge with many arches that carries, a road, railway or water over low-lying ground.

BOOKS TO READ

The Rough Guide to Italy (Rough Guides, 2016)

Lonely Planet Italy (Travel Guide) by Cristian Bonetto (Lonely Planet, 2016)

Eyewitness Travel Guide: Italy (Dorling Kindersley, 2017)

Eyewitness Top 10 Travel Guide: Florence & Tuscany (Dorling Kindersley, 2016)

Eyewitness Top 10 Travel Guide: Venice (Dorling Kindersley, 2016)

Unpacked: Italy by Clive Gifford (Wayland, 2014)

Been There: Italy by Annabel Savery (Franklin Watts, 2014)

WEBSITES

http://www.roughguides.com/destinations/europe/italy/

The Rough Guide to Italy website is packed with interesting and useful information for your visit to Italy. There are tips on where and when to travel, including lots of great itineraries to inspire your own journey.

http://www.lonelyplanet.com/italy

Lonely Planet's website is a great introduction to Italy and tells you about the best places to visit, historical and geographical information, food and drink to sample, and practical hints and tips about money, health, language and local customs.

http://travel.michelin.com/web/destination/Italy

This website from Michelin provides all the information you'll need for a fascinating and safe journey around Italy. Follow some alternative travel routes, take your pick from loads of travel activities and check out the best places to stay.

https://www.gov.uk/foreign-travel-advice/italy

It's always a good idea to check out the official government advice before you make any journey abroad. You can find out the latest news and information about Italy on this UK government website.

Note to parents and teachers:
Every effort has been made by the Publishers to ensure that the websites in this book are suitable for children, that they are of the highest educational value, and that they contain no inappropriate or offensive material. However, because of the nature of the Internet, it is impossible to guarantee that the contents of these sites will not be altered. We strongly advise that Internet access is supervised by a responsible adult.

INDEX